S0-BIQ-729

ENGLISH WIT

QUIPS AND QUOTES

Tom Hay

summersdale

ENGLISH WIT

First published in 2009
New edition published in 2012
This edition copyright © Summersdale Publishers Ltd, 2012

Summersdale Publishers Ltd
46 West Street
Chichester
West Sussex
PO19 1RP
UK

www.summersdale.com

Printed and bound in China

ISBN: 978-1-84953-305-8

Substantial discounts on bulk quantities of Summersdale books are available to corporations, professional associations and other organisations. For details telephone Summersdale Publishers on (+44-1243-771107), fax (+44-1243-786300) or email (nicky@summersdale.com).

CONTENTS

EDITOR'S NOTE

The English can always be relied upon to conjure up an off-the-cuff quip to rescue a potentially awkward situation – even the Queen Mother, who after choking on a fish bone retorted, 'The salmon have got their own back.'

They are also renowned for their deadpan delivery and are not averse to friendly jibes about their unique quirks and foibles: take George Mikes' observation of the English obsession for queuing, or John Cleese's comment on his fellow countrymen's lack of culinary skill, for example.

So now it's time to hang up your bowler hat, uncurl that stiff upper lip and indulge in this laugh-out-loud compendium. With quotes from the likes of Eddie Izzard, Jo Brand and William Shakespeare, it's guaranteed to tickle your funny bone.

LOVE AND MARRIAGE

Marry an archaeologist.
The older you get, the
more interested he
is in you.

AGATHA CHRISTIE

Love is like the measles; we all have to go through it.

JEROME K. JEROME

I am a very committed wife. And I should be committed – for being married so many times.

ELIZABETH TAYLOR

I can still enjoy sex at 74 – I live at 75 so it's no distance.

BOB MONKHOUSE

What do I look for in women?
Clean knickers.

MICHAEL CAINE

I thought coq au vin was
love in a lorry.

VICTORIA WOOD

As usual, there is a great woman
behind every idiot.

JOHN LENNON

I'm a believer in safe sex. I put a handrail round the bed.

KEN DODD

Scientists have discovered a food
that reduces a woman's sex drive
by 99 per cent. Wedding cake.

JIM DAVIDSON

For our wedding anniversary I
took my wife to the pub. She told
me I should buy something for
the house so I did – a round
of drinks.

BENNY HILL

The penalty for getting the woman you want is that you must keep her.

LYTTON STRACHEY

Modern drugs are wonderful. They enable a wife with pneumonia to nurse her husband through the flu.

JILLY COOPER

When a man opens the car door
for his wife, it's either a new car
or a new wife.

PRINCE PHILIP, DUKE OF EDINBURGH

To fall in love you have to be in
the state of mind for it to take,
like a disease.

NANCY MITFORD

EATING
AND
DRINKING

Life's too short to stuff a mushroom.

SHIRLEY CONRAN

I won't eat anything
that has intelligent
life, but I'd gladly eat a
network executive or
a politician.

MARTY FELDMAN

The English contribution to world cuisine – the chip.

JOHN CLEESE

Good apple pies are a considerable part of our domestic happiness.

JANE AUSTEN

Vegetarianism is harmless
enough, though it is apt to
fill a man with wind and
self-righteousness.

ROBERT HUTCHINSON

Music with dinner is an insult both
to the cook and the violinist.

G. K. CHESTERTON

Enclosing every thin man, there's
a fat man demanding elbow room.

EVELYN WAUGH

The salmon have got their
own back.

THE QUEEN MOTHER,
AFTER CHOKING ON A FISH BONE

Coffee in England always tastes like a chemistry experiment.

AGATHA CHRISTIE

ENGLAND AND THE ENGLISH

If the English language made any sense, lackadaisical would have something to do with a shortage of flowers.

DOUG LARSON

An Englishman, even if he is alone,
forms an orderly queue of one.

GEORGE MIKES

The difference between English
and American humour is
$150 a minute.

ERIC IDLE

I like the English. They have
the most rigid code of immorality
in the world.

MALCOLM BRADBURY

What a pity it is that we have
no amusements in England but
vice and religion!

SYDNEY SMITH

We English are good at forgiving
our enemies; it releases us from
the obligation of liking our friends.

P. D. JAMES

Mad dogs and Englishmen go out
in the midday sun.

NOËL COWARD

The English never draw a line
without blurring it.

WINSTON CHURCHILL

But Lord! To see the absurd nature
of the Englishmen, that cannot
forbear laughing and jeering at
everything that looks strange.

SAMUEL PEPYS

How amazing that the language of a few thousand savages living on a fog-encrusted island in the North Sea should become the language of the world.

NORMAN ST JOHN-STEVAS

The English winter – ending in July to recommence in August.

LORD BYRON

If you have a high-powered car to drive around in it's like a roundabout.

WILL SELF ON BRITAIN BEING TOO SMALL

WORK AND MONEY

I like work: it fascinates me. I can sit and look at it for hours.

JEROME K. JEROME

If you can't get a job as a pianist in a brothel you become a royal reporter.

MAX HASTINGS

Having money is rather like being a blonde. It is more fun but not vital.

MARY QUANT

I love deadlines. I especially like the whooshing sound they make as they go flying by.

DOUGLAS ADAMS

The avoidance of taxes is the only intellectual pursuit that carries any reward.

JOHN MAYNARD KEYNES

There are three
ways of losing money:
racing is the quickest,
women the most
pleasant, and farming
the most certain.

LORD AMHERST

I told the Inland Revenue I didn't owe them a penny because I lived near the seaside.

KEN DODD

The employer generally gets the employees he deserves.

WALTER RALEIGH

When an actor comes to me and wants to discuss his character, I say, 'It's in the script.' If he says, 'But what's my motivation?' I say, 'Your salary.'

ALFRED HITCHCOCK

Borrow fivers off everyone.

RICHARD BRANSON'S ANSWER TO THE QUESTION 'WHAT IS THE QUICKEST WAY TO BECOME A MILLIONAIRE?'

The only reason I made a commercial for American Express was to pay for my American Express bill.

PETER USTINOV

SPORT

This bowler's like my dog: three short legs and balls that swing each way.

BRIAN JOHNSTON

I used to play football when I was young but then my eyes went bad – so I became a referee.

ERIC MORECAMBE

Golf should never be played on a day with a 'y' in it.

LES DAWSON

I don't make mistakes. I make
prophecies which immediately
turn out to be wrong.

MURRAY WALKER

When God gave Paul Gascoigne
his enormous footballing talent,
he took his brain out at the same
time to even things up.

TONY BANKS

Oh God! If there be cricket in heaven let there also be rain.

ALEC DOUGLAS-HOME

The Oxford rowing crew – eight minds with but a single thought, if that.

MAX BEERBOHM

Winning is everything. The only ones who remember you when you come second are your wife and your dog.

DAMON HILL

One way to stop a runaway horse is to bet on him.

JEFFREY BERNARD

I was watching sumo wrestling on the television for two hours before I realised it was darts.

HATTIE HAYRIDGE

When I first heard about Viagra, I thought it was a new player Chelsea had just signed.

TONY BANKS

OLD AGE

You know you're
getting old when the
girl you smile at thinks
you're one of her
father's friends.

ALAN MURRAY

As you get older three things happen. The first is your memory goes, and I can't remember the other two...

NORMAN WISDOM

I don't need you to remind me of my old age, I have a bladder to do that for me.

STEPHEN FRY

Once it was impossible to find any Bond villains older than myself, I retired.

ROGER MOORE

I knew I was going bald when it was taking longer and longer to wash my face.

HARRY HILL

The only thing for old age is a brave face, a good tailor and comfortable shoes.

ALAN AYCKBOURN

I attribute my great age to the simple fact that I was born a very long time ago.

JOHN GIELGUD

I'm 59 and people call me middle-aged. How many 118-year-old men do you know?

BARRY CRYER

I am getting to an age when I can only enjoy the last sport left. It is called hunting for your spectacles.

SIR EDWARD GREY

I'm getting on. I'm now equipped with a snooze button.

DENIS NORDEN

Growing old is compulsory, growing up is optional.

BOB MONKHOUSE

My grandmother is 92 years old
and she hasn't a single grey hair.
She's bald.

BERNARD MANNING

The older I get, the older old is.

TOM BAKER

One day you look in the mirror and realise the face you are shaving is your father's.

ROBERT HARRIS

POLITICS

In politics, if you want
anything said, ask
a man. If you want
something done, ask
a woman.

MARGARET THATCHER

The House of Commons is the longest running farce in the West End.

CYRIL SMITH

She can't see an institution without hitting it with her handbag.

JULIAN CRITCHLEY ON MARGARET THATCHER

Tony Blair puts two poems in
a bus shelter and calls
it a university.

VICTORIA WOOD

The ability to foretell what is
going to happen tomorrow, next
week, next month and next year.
And to have the ability afterwards
to explain why it didn't happen.

WINSTON CHURCHILL ON THE NECESSARY
QUALITIES TO BE A POLITICIAN

The proper memory for a politician is one that knows what to remember and what to forget.

JOHN MORLEY

I remain just one thing, and one thing only, and that is a clown. It places me on a far higher plane than any politician.

CHARLIE CHAPLIN

Anybody who enjoys being in the House of Commons probably needs psychiatric care.

KEN LIVINGSTONE

PREPOSTEROUS
PONDERINGS

I am patient with
stupidity but not
with those who are
proud of it.

EDITH SITWELL

Dontopedology is the science of opening your mouth and putting your foot in it. I've been practising it for years.

PRINCE PHILIP, DUKE OF EDINBURGH

I have a stepladder. It's a very nice stepladder but it's sad that I never knew my real ladder.

CRAIG CHARLES

Honolulu – it's got everything.
Sand for the children, sun for the
wife, sharks for the wife's mother.

KEN DODD

If you could build a house on
a trampoline, that would
suit me fine.

ALAN RICKMAN

I have a memory like an elephant.
In fact, elephants often
consult me.

NOËL COWARD

My idea of heaven is eating
pâté de fois gras to the sound
of trumpets.

SYDNEY SMITH

INSULTS

I see her as one
great stampede of lips
directed at the nearest
derrière.

NOËL COWARD

I never comment on referees and
I'm not going to break the habit of
a lifetime for that prat.

RON ATKINSON

She tells enough white lies to
ice a wedding cake.

MARGOT ASQUITH

The tautness of his face
sours ripe grapes.

WILLIAM SHAKESPEARE

She looked as if she had been
poured into her clothes and
forgotten to say when.

P. G. WODEHOUSE

Alan Shearer is so dull he once
made the papers for having
a one-in-a-bed romp.

NICK HANCOCK

Is it always his desire to give his
imitation of a semi-house-trained
polecat?

MICHAEL FOOT ON NORMAN TEBBIT

Sir, you are like a pin, but without either its head or point.

DOUGLAS JERROLD

Never before in the history of
fashion has so little material been
raised so high to reveal so much
that needs to be covered so badly.

CECIL BEATON ON THE MINISKIRT

You've got the subtlety
of a bullfrog.

H. G. WELLS

The right honourable gentleman is reminiscent of a poker. The only difference is that a poker gives off the occasional signs of warmth.

BENJAMIN DISRAELI ON ROBERT PEEL

THE BIG
SLEEP

I get my daily paper,
look at the obituaries
page and if I'm not
there I carry on
as usual.

PATRICK MOORE

The idea is to die young as
late as possible.

ASHLEY MONTAGU

All men are cremated equal.

BEN ELTON

I blame myself for my boyfriend's death. I shot him.

JO BRAND

In Liverpool, the difference between a funeral and a wedding is one less drunk.

PAUL O'GRADY

When I get in a taxi, the first thing they say is, 'Hello Eric, I thought you were dead.'

ERIC SYKES

I am ready to meet my Maker. Whether my Maker is ready for the ordeal of meeting me is another matter.

WINSTON CHURCHILL

When someone close to you dies,
move seats.

JIMMY CARR

There's nothing glorious in dying.
Anyone can do it.

JOHN LYDON (AKA JOHNNY ROTTEN)

If you don't go to other people's funerals, they won't go to yours.

BOB MONKHOUSE

THE ARTS

There's no money in poetry, but then there's no poetry in money, either.

ROBERT GRAVES

Writing is easy. You only need to
stare at a piece of blank paper
until your forehead bleeds.

DOUGLAS ADAMS

Acting is merely the art of
keeping a large group of people
from coughing.

RALPH RICHARDSON

Art consists of limitation. The most beautiful part of every picture is the frame.

G. K. CHESTERTON

The moral of film-making in Britain is that you will be screwed by the weather.

HUGH GRANT

I'm a skilled, professional actor. Whether or not I've any talent is beside the point.

MICHAEL CAINE

[It] is like asking a lamp post how it feels about dogs.

CHRISTOPHER HAMPTON ON ASKING A WRITER WHAT HE THINKS ABOUT CRITICS

The length of a film should be directly related to the endurance of the human bladder.

ALFRED HITCHCOCK

The media. It sounds like a convention of spiritualists.

TOM STOPPARD

A great many people employed reading and writing would be better employed keeping rabbits.

EDITH SITWELL

A book may be compared to your neighbour; if it be good, it cannot last too long; if bad, you cannot get rid of it too early.

RUPERT BROOKE

WISE
WORDS

Never put a sock in a toaster.

EDDIE IZZARD

The only way to be sure of catching a train is to miss the one before it.

G. K. CHESTERTON

If you can't be a good example, then you'll just have to be a horrible warning.

CATHERINE AIRD

Good but rarely came from good advice.

LORD BYRON

Time is an illusion, lunchtime doubly so.

DOUGLAS ADAMS

Laugh and the world laughs with you. Snore and you sleep alone.

ANTHONY BURGESS

Never keep up with the Joneses. Drag them down to your level. It's cheaper.

QUENTIN CRISP

It is a good thing for
an uneducated man
to read books of
quotations.

WINSTON CHURCHILL

If you're interested in finding out
more about our humour books, follow us
on Twitter: @SummersdaleLOL

www.summersdale.com